Pastoral address of the Genesee Annual Conference of the Methodist Episcopal Church, adopted at its session in Perry, New York, October 20, 1858

Attributed to
Israel Chamberlayne

First Fruits Press
Wilmore, Kentucky
c2017

Pastoral address of the Genesee Annual Conference of the Methodist Episcopal Church, adopted at its session in Perry, New York, October 20, 1858.
Attributed to Israel Chamberlayne.

First Fruits Press, ©2017
Previously published by H.H. Otis, 1858

ISBN: 9781621716464 (print), 9781621716471 (digital), 9781621716488 (kindle)

Digital version at http://place.asburyseminary.edu/freemethodistbooks/26/

For all other uses, contact:

First Fruits Press
B.L. Fisher Library
Asbury Theological Seminary
204 N. Lexington Ave.
Wilmore, KY 40390
http://place.asburyseminary.edu/firstfruits

Chamberlayne, Israel, 1795-1875.
    Pastoral address of the Genesee Annual Conference of the Methodist Episcopal Church, adopted at its session in Perry, New York, October 20, 1858 / [Israel Chamberlayne].--Wilmore, Kentucky : First Fruits Press, ©2017.
        14 pages; 21 cm.
        Reprint. Previously published: Buffalo, [New York] : H.H. Otis, 1858.
        ISBN - 13: 9781621716464 (pbk.)
        1. Methodist Episcopal Church--Sermons. 2. Sermons, American. 3. Church—Unity—Sermons. 4. Public worship—Sermons.   I. Title. II. Methodist Episcopal Church. Genesee Conference.
BX8235.C52 2017

Cover design by Jon Ramsay

asburyseminary.edu
800.2ASBURY
204 North Lexington Avenue
Wilmore, Kentucky 40390

First Fruits
THE ACADEMIC OPEN PRESS OF ASBURY SEMINARY

First Fruits Press

The Academic Open Press of Asbury Theological Seminary
204 N. Lexington Ave., Wilmore, KY 40390
859-858-2236
first.fruits@asburyseminary.edu
asbury.to/firstfruits

Pastoral Address

OF THE

GENESEE ANNUAL CONFERENCE

OF THE

Methodist Episcopal Church,

ADOPTED

AT ITS SESSION IN PERRY, NEW YORK,

October 20, 1858.

———— ◆•◆ ————

BUFFALO:
PUBLISHED BY H. H. OTIS, 226 MAIN STREET.
1858.

PASTORAL ADDRESS

OF THE

GENESEE ANNUAL CONFERENCE

OF THE

𝕸𝖊𝖙𝖍𝖔𝖉𝖎𝖘𝖙 𝕰𝖕𝖎𝖘𝖈𝖔𝖕𝖆𝖑 𝕮𝖍𝖚𝖗𝖈𝖍.

ADOPTED AT ITS SESSION IN PERRY, N. Y., OCTOBER 20th, 1858.

———————•———————

BELOVED BRETHREN:

Custom has long sanctioned the practice of pastoral addresses, wherein the overseers of the Lord's flock, from time to time, lay before the people of their charge, those subjects of common interest on which the unity and prosperity of the church depend.

While pastors and people are embraced in one common interest, and derive their spiritual and ecclesiastical prosperity from sources common to both, yet, each have their peculiar duties, on the faithful discharge of which the glory and permanency of our common Zion instrumentally depend. We, as pastors, are called to take heed to all the flock over which the Holy Ghost hath made us overseers; to perform toward them the office of a shepherd according to our Lord's command, viz., to "feed,"—to take care of—both the lambs and the sheep. We need not declare to you, beloved brethren, that we desire to watch for your souls as those who must give account, taking the oversight of you, not by constraint, but willingly; not as being lords over God's heritage, but as ensamples to the flock. Nor need we say, that we should prove ourselves but hirelings, and not true shepherds, if we see danger approaching, and give no alarm, or if we forbear our timely and affectionate advice and admonition.

In all times, and in all conditions, the true prosperity of the church must arise from her *unity*—unity between pastors and people, and unity between all the parts of the membership. And we beg, first of all, to call your attention to this duty, so pointedly and so repeatedly laid down in sacred scripture. The dying Savior and Head of the Church has prayed, and, in that prayer, has laid down the fundamental duty of church members,—"that they all might be one,"—that they might be one in the Father and in the Son—"that the world might believe that Jesus is the very Christ." The holy apostle prays: "Now, I beseech you, brethren, by the name of our Lord Jesus Christ, that ye all speak the same thing, and that there be no divisions among you; but that ye be perfectly joined together, in the same mind, and in the same judgment." Again he prays: "Now, the God of patience and consolation, grant you to be like-minded, one toward another, according to Christ Jesus, that ye may, with one mind and one mouth, glorify God." "Fulfill ye my joy," says he, "that ye be like-minded, having the same love, being of one accord, of one mind."

From such solemn and earnest admonitions, as well as from the nature of the case, we may see that, in the eyes of God, no church can be prosperous which is not united. But we especially call your attention to the point, that it is the first duty of the church member, as well as of the minister, to avoid all occasions of difference with brethren, and to "follow after the things which make for peace, and things whereby one may edify another." If peace and unity are fundamentally necessary to the prosperity, not to say the existence, of the church, then the moral of the subject would teach, that we have no right to disturb that peace, for any less reason than would authorize us to overturn and destroy the whole church. And, brethren, we call to your minds the covenant you ratified with the body of the church, when you entered her communion. That covenant is still in force. It is of the nature of a solemn, personal contract to conform to one standard of doctrine, discipline, and fellowship with the church, while your membership remains. O, if pastors and people could realize all the weight of this primary duty, and the fearful iniquity of dividing the members of Christ's body, in heart and judgment, it might then be written of us, as of the church of old, "Then had the churches rest throughout all Judea, and Galilee and Samaria, and were edified; and, walking in the fear of the Lord, and in the comfort of Holy Ghost, were multiplied."

In order to our greater union, and better understanding, we would call your attention to a few particulars.

And, first, the subject of Christian Holiness. We rejoice at every method and instrumentality of calling the attention of the church and the world, to the nature and obligations of a holy life. Without this, neither churches nor institutions will be of saving benefit to mankind. It is the grand ultimate result of mediatorial merit and agency, and of all heaven-appointed instrumentalities. In this we all agree, that "without holiness no man shall see the Lord;" that holiness of heart, victory over all sin, renewal in the complete image of God, is attainable in this life; that it is all by grace, through faith; that it is the work of the Holy Spirit; and that it is the privilege and duty of every believer. We further agree, also, in marking the distinction between a *babe* in Christ, and a *man* in Christ; between the first principle of Christian doctrine and experience, and the perfect state, or the measure of the stature of the fullness of Christ. We all believe that the remains of evil, together with a general, comparative feebleness of the graces, belong to the state of childhood in Christ; while the opposite belong to the mature and perfect state.

We further agree in adopting one discipline and form of government. So far as principles and essential forms of church government are concerned, we have, happily, no controversy.

One other matter we will mention, which is not less important to our unity than either doctrine or discipline, in which we are also agreed: that point is, the spirit and life of Methodism. We all agree that Christianity is a principle of divine life in the soul, and that the spirit and soul of Methodism is the life of God in the hearts of its members. We heartily adopt the definition which Mr. Wesley gives the people called Methodists, viz., that "they are no other than a company of men, having the form and seeking the power of godliness."

In view of these essential and fundamental points of agreement, we ask, How can it be that we should widely differ? Brethren, it is not on essential points that we differ; it is on modes, and accidents, and circumstantial forms.

For instance, we differ in the conduct of prayer meetings. It is but too well known that differences on this subject have been the occasion in various places, from which have arisen controversies as determined, as if the very existence of Methodism, and of Christianity itself, were depending. But why, we ask you, brethren, should there be any dispute, much less division, on this ground? Surely there cannot, provided, that, in the spirit of the gospel of peace, we are willing to be satisfied with what has been matter of long and well established usage.

These meetings, limited as to time and place in the discretion of the pastors, are always free to all our members; who are subject to no restraint, unless in cases where rights are claimed which cannot be allowed without touching upon the rights of others. We have always been accustomed, upon proper occasion, to invite seekers of salvation to the altar for prayers. So far as we know, the expediency of this is just as unquestioned now, as ever heretofore. Nor, though less known, and less generally approved, do we feel disposed to disallow the practice of encouraging those to come to the altar for prayers, who desire the blessing of a clean heart,—provided it be done without reflecting directly or indirectly upon those who do not choose to come; and, provided finally, that every such proceeding be *under pastoral direction*.

You will permit us, also, beloved brethren, in this connection, to refer to the matter of singing in our public meetings; than which, few subjects have been more prolific of dissensions among us. For such a mode as makes this sacred service a monopoly with the choir, the spirit and usages of Methodism have no sympathy. If such usage exist in any of our assemblies, we earnestly advise our ministers and people, to induce its discontinuance, with all prudence, but with all fidelity. "Let all in our congregations be exhorted to sing—not one in ten only."

If, on the other hand, there are any among us, who are in the habit of stirring up contention against congregational singing under a disciplined and competent leadership, whether such leadership be constituted by few or many, we would admonish them that "we have no such custom, nor has the church of God."

In addressing you thus familiarly and earnestly, our duty to you, personally, as well as our regard for the prosperity of our beloved Zion, requires, that we speak of a subject of much greater delicacy than those which we have named above. We refer to the matter of *physical demonstrations* in our sacred assemblies—bodily contortions, falling, leaping, clapping, screaming, and such like. Of these, we hazard nothing in the remark, that they are entirely at variance with the law of the New Testament, which has its embodiment in the precept, "Let all things be done decently and in order." From the time of Mr. Wesley to this present time, the representative men of Methodism, the wisest and holiest,—Coke, Clarke, Watson, Hedding, Emory, Fisk, Olin,—have regarded these things, not as matters to be encouraged, but to be repressed; wisely and gently, to be sure, but still to be repressed; as being, not only not adapted to promote the work of God, though often appearing in connection with it, but as being detrimental and disgraceful to it.

As to Mr. Wesley himself, and how he judged and acted, with respect to this class of excesses, it were better, in place of any mere statement of ours, that he should be allowed to speak for himself. How nearly the extravagances of his time, have occasionally been reproduced in our own, and what mode of treatment is most in accordance with his treatment, will appear from the following quotations:

To Adam Clarke, within five months of his death, he writes, Vol. VII, p. 206:

"In the great revival in London, my first difficulty was to bring in temper those who opposed the work; and my next, to check and regulate the extravagances of those who promoted it. *And this was by far the hardest part of the work;* for many of them would bear no check at all. But I followed one rule, though with all calmness—'You must either *bend* or *break.*' Beware of jealousies, or judging one another. Never think a man is an enemy to the work, because he reproves irregularities."

To his brother Charles, concerning the work in London, he writes, Vol VI, p. 664:

"For eighteen or twenty days, I *heard,* but rarely opened my mouth. I think I now understand the affair, at least as well as any person in England. The sum is this: 1. The meeting at Beech Lane, before I came to town, was a *bear-garden,* full of noise, brawling, cursing, swearing, blasphemy, and confusion. 2. Those who *prayed* were partly the occasion of this, by their horrid screaming, and unscriptural enthusiastic expressions. 3. Being determined to *mend* or *end* them, I removed the meeting to the Foundry. 4. Immediately the noise, brawling, cursing, swearing, blasphemy, and confusion ceased. 5. There was less and less screaming, and less unscriptural and enthusiastic language."

Again, in Vol. IV, p. 631, he says:

"It is chiefly among these enormous mountains that so many have been perfected in love. But even while they are full of love, Satan strives to persuade many to extravagance. This appears: 1. Frequently *three or four, yea, ten or twelve,* pray aloud together. 2. Some of them, perhaps *many,* scream all together *as loud as they possibly can.* 3. Some of them use improper, yea, indecent expressions in prayer. 4. *Several drop down as dead,* and are as stiff as a corpse; but, in a while, they start up and cry '*Glory! Glory!*' perhaps twenty or thirty times together. Just so do the French prophets, and, very lately, the *Jumpers* in Wales—bringing the *real work into contempt.*"

On this subject, we have already referred you, brethren, to the law of the New Testament. We also, appeal from any supposed evidence for these irregularities, to that law of our natures which, inasmuch as God is no less the author of our nature and its laws, than of the bible, and the law of the bible is entitled to be regarded as of collateral authority on this question. We refer to that *instinctive sense* which God has imbedded in the constitution of every human soul—the *Sense of Propriety.* To what, but to the arbitrament of this sense, does the apostle bring that question, as to what was fitting and proper in the demeanor of christian women: "Does not *nature* itself teach you," thus and so?

When, therefore, the question arises whether, in social or public worship,

one, or a dozen, should exhort or pray at once, how dead or deaf to the
sense in question, must be that mind which does not hear and heed the echo
of His voice, who is denominated " not the author of confusion, but of order,
as in all the churches;" and who elsewhere teaches us, in His written word,
what He has also taught us by this sense of propriety—this perception of
the fitness of things—that public and social worship are to be conducted
with regard to the common edification, as their true and only end; and,
consequently, whatever impairs its adaptation to that end, is, so far an utter
perversion of the institution itself.

God's revealed and natural laws are harmonious. If the mind is instinct-
ively repulsed by exhibitions of disorder and confusion in the worship of
God, it only shows that it is under the control of that law which the divine
hand has written in every human heart.

And, inasmuch as the influence of the Divine Spirit can never contravene
these laws—the revealed and the natural—it follows,

1. That in public or social meetings, no one can be led by a *Divine*
influence to infract the law of order. " The spirit of the prophets is subject
to the prophets."

2. That the Spirit never contradicts the natural proprieties of life, nor
any of the natural and reasonable conventionalities of society. So that,
whether in the social circle, or in the social prayer-meeting, " Charity doth
not behave itself unseemly," i. e., *indecently.*

A *true scriptural* fervor in devotion then, brethren, is distinguished from
that which is *false*, by the fact that the one is modified and limited by the
law of the New Testament, having its counterpart, as we have seen, in that
other law of our natures, enforcing the decencies, fitnesses and proprieties
of life; while the other contemns all law, save that of its own ungoverned
impulses.

This latter is what we mean, and what Mr. Wesley means, by *Enthusiasm;* some of the various phases of which we have noticed above, and
which, with immaterial variations, are occasionally manifest among us, to
the just offense of every enlightened, christian mind, and the no small dis-
honor of Methodism in the eyes of all *right-minded thinking men.* In pass-
ing from this topic of admonition, you will allow us, with Mr. Wesley, to
say that, " the reproach of *Christ* we are willing to bear, but not the
reproach of *enthusiasm,* if we can help it."

Closely allied to this, christian brethren, is another evil, against which it
is our duty to guard you, as we should deprecate its ruinous effects upon
yourselves,—as we hope to render our own account with joy in the day of
the Lord Jesus,—and as we would be mindful of our covenant vow, to " be

ready, with all diligence, to banish and drive away all erroneous and strange doctrines contrary to God's word."

The evil referred to, is *Fanaticism*. That it is quite limited as yet, we are thankful to know. That it truly exists, however, we are constrained to believe. What *we* mean by *Fanaticism* is,

1. The supposition of being under the *immediate guidance of the Holy Spirit* in matters of duty, and particularly as to conduct in seasons of worship. Our church, following Mr. Wesley, and all our standard writers, has ever stood in utter opposition to this dangerous delusion. For proof of this, we must, for want of space, refer you, for correct information, to the sources already noticed, as also for the just relation which the Holy Spirit holds to the Sacred Word, their respective offices, and the true interpretation of those texts which are perverted to the support of the fundamental error in question.

Whoever dreams of an inspiration other than that of the bible—an inspiration revealing truth and teaching duty—will be quite sure to have revelations enough. If a preacher, he will be wiser than all the presiding elders, and all the bishops; if a private member, he will be far above the need of the advice or admonition of his pastor. This, then, is what *we* mean, and what all enlightened christendom means, by *fanaticism*.

2. Made equal, in one respect, to prophets and apostles, the subject of this disordered imagination, very naturally comes to suppose himself their rival in another. He is a discerner of spirits. Why not? If the secrets of the *Divine* Mind are open to his perception, what vail should hide from his gaze the secrets of the *human* soul? Here, then, is what we regard, and what the christian world regards, as another well defined type of *fanaticism*.

Naturally as the birth of this twin hallucination accompanies the other, we should scarcely have called it to your attention, but for the notoriety of the historic fact, that, at no period, nor among any class of visionaries, has either of them made its advent alone.

Nor does the present time appear to furnish any exception to the general rule. That christians are now occasionally taught to expect the possession of the faculty of discovering the religious state of those with whom they are brought into contact, we have reason to know. That some among us claim its possession, we are also persuaded. Nor is it less, but even more abundantly evident, that still greater numbers are in the habit of pronouncing anything but flattering decisions upon the piety and integrity of their brethren, in a manner hardly explicable, and certainly not to be justified, on any other supposition, than that of their being able to pry within those folds which veil the heart from all ordinary human scrutiny.

And what, you will do well, brethren, to ask yourselves, is more exactly adapted to flatter the corrupt propensities of the human soul, than the insane conceit of its endowment with such a wealth of superhuman attainment; especially, its pride of superior intelligence, its pride of superior holiness? Was not the former the downfall of an archangel? And have we not seen the latter—the conceit of a sanctity entitling it to bear the standard before ranks of admiring followers—have we not seen it quenching the aspirations of the standard bearer in the foul vapors of sensualism, and trailing his standard in dishonorable dust? Here is the "depth of Satan." Let us *beware*.

3. A third trait of the fanaticism to which we refer, and one which denotes its utter incongruity with the religion of the New Testament, is malevolence, — vindictiveness, vituperation, evil speaking, scandal-mongery, whispering, backbiting, swellings, tumults. Fanaticism, as distinguished from Enthusiasm, is often characterized by malevolence; a sure evidence that its origin is not from above, but from beneath.

We are free to admit, however, that liability to malevolence is by no means peculiar to those who are most inclined to excesses in religion. It is but too possible to attempt the correction of such excesses in a spirit utterly opposed to the loving mind that was in Christ. For the sake of the souls of our brethren, as well as our own, let us beware of such a spirit; for it is not of God—it can only lead to evil.

4. You will permit us, dearly beloved, to call your attention to yet another phase of the evil under consideration. An apostle exhorts us to try the spirits. By what standard? The word of God, responded to, as we have noted above, by those natural and universal sentiments of fitness and propriety which God has interwoven in the constitution of every human mind, "To the law and the testimony: if they speak not according to these, it is because there is no light in them." What, then, we ask you, does this law of our nature, and that law of God, teach us on the subject of *regard for reputation?*

The doctrine taught by some, and believed and practised by others, is, that a right religious state is attested by an utter indifference to the estimation in which we are held by others. By easy consequence, if not asserted in terms, it comes to this: that whether society regards a christian man as honest or dishonest, or a christian woman as chaste or unchaste, is to be with both, or either, a thing of perfect indifference. Hence it is, that whosoever abides this test is admitted to be sincere, whether as a seeker of pardon or holiness, or as a professor of holiness. On the other hand, he who does not approve himself by this criterion, is allowed a claim to but little, if any, further advance in divine illumination than that of him who saw "men as trees walking."

Hence it is, also, that, not satisfied with mere indifference to social consideration, the earnest christian is induced to *direct efforts* to cheapen and scandalize himself in the eyes of the world, and to question his claim to the christian character, till he has the evidence that "all men speak ill of him."

Brethren, need we say to you *this is all wrong?* Doubtless our characters and our lives should be yielded up, if, in the providence of God, it fall out that such a sacrifice is the only alternative by which we can preserve our fidelity to Christ, and save our souls. But are not our characters even dearer than our lives? If, then, to throw away the latter, be a suicidal sin, is not the voluntary sacrifice of the former a sin still more suicidal? Recklessness of reputation, as a mere speculative affair, were startling enough. But of this, as such, we do not speak. We earnestly admonish you against it, in view of its practical application. Do we not see it employed in enacting, and exciting others to enact, the wildest and most revolting of those scenes which offend the day and make night hideous? For illustration, if you have not witnessed any of those scenes, we refer you again to some of their prototypes as drawn by the pen of the sainted Wesley.

Such is its spirit, and such are some only, of its manifestations. We are happy to state, that, comparatively speaking, by far the most of our societies have escaped this infection altogether. And, as it was with the church in Sardis, where it does predominate, even there, there are, in some places at least, a *few* names who have not defiled their garments; while, with regard to other portions of our work, pervaded by the same vitiating and disorganizing influence, there are *many* such names, walking like the Hebrews, "unhurt in the midst of the fire," and, who, if still faithful, shall walk with Christ "in white, for they are worthy."

Be assured, brethren, that God's spirit just as truly leads us to be careful of our reputation, as our natural instincts lead us to preserve our lives. A reputation wholly consecrated to God, should, for His sake, be most jealously preserved. If we are reckless of what the world may say or think of us, we show ourselves to be without the spirit. Our influence with others is our only power to do them good. Bankrupt in character, we are worse than dead. He who neither has, nor wishes the respect of the society in which he lives, is a dangerous character in that society.

A few of the many expressions of the mind of our great Head, on this subject, are: "Shun the appearance of evil,"—"Walk in wisdom toward them that are without,"—"A bishop must have a good report from them that are without,"—"Give no offense in any thing, that the ministry be not blamed,"—"I please all men for their good to edification,"—"I become all things to all men,"—"Let your light *so* shine before men that they may glorify your Father who is in heaven."

Your careful consideration of what has been said on this subject, will enable you to mark the utter disagreement of the spirit and fruits of these wild and extravagant notions in religion, with the spirit and legitimate workings of an evangelically spiritual religion.

If, brethren, our hearts' desire and prayer to God for you, are realized, you will eschew the evils of which we have admonished you. You will not give countenance to novelties in doctrine, and modes of operation. While gently bearing with, you will labor to repress all violent and unseemly excesses. You will turn away from all pretensions and pretenders as to direct revelations and discernment of spirits. You will leave all such vain dreams to the devotees of Mormonism and the followers of Andrew Jackson Davis. Or, if any, professing the faith of Wesley, still prate such stupid nonsense, and will not be admonished, let them know, through the proper official medium, that they have no more place among us.

And, beloved brethren, we are constrained to say the same with respect to those who, remaining in our fellowship, and enjoying its ministrations and ordinances, leave the burdens of supporting the church to those who love it well enough to pay their own quotas together with those of delinquent brethren,—while they, the delinquents, satisfy their mistaken consciences by exciting insubordination and "enjoying" religion.

Such conduct is a violation of the whole spirit and meaning of our Methodistic economy. Most of those who have been misled into these wide departures from the plainest principles of ecclesiastic and gospel duty, will, we are charitably persuaded, see and feel the error of their way, and return to the only course of action which can render their continuance with us, a blessing either to us or to themselves.

Bear with us, beloved, while we speak of another class of evils more or less observable in some departments of our work. We have noted, with no small concern, that, in various ways, a disposition is manifested to institute and maintain religious services independent of, and contrary to, the counsel and disciplinary authority of those having the pastoral charge where such services are held. This, both in principle and effect, tends to nothing less than the practical subversion of our whole polity, inasmuch, as by setting aside the pastoral office, as to the exercise of its constituted and just prerogatives, it destroys the only bond by which our characteristic organism can be held together.

Not to express our disapproval of all such irregularities, and admonish their discontinuance wherever they exist, were to show ourselves recreant to the most sacred of our obligations. We have no hesitation in admitting, that the occasional appointment of a social meeting, without direct reference to the preacher in charge, has always been practised. And the same remark holds with reference to an occasional sermon by one preacher within the pastoral limits of another. But all such cases have had their justification in a reasonable presumption, that the pastor, had he been consulted, would have yielded his cheerful consent.

But for our private members to assume the appointment and control of religious meetings, in direct opposition, not only to the known wishes, but to the explicit advice and remonstrance of the pastor, is an innovation of which we must utterly disapprove, and from which we would most affectionately and earnestly dissuade you. These practices, we are thankful to acknowledge, are far from being extensive. We beseech those who have been inconsiderately betrayed into them, or either of them, to return to our established and only safe usage in these matters.

Our solemn conviction of duty obliges us to express, also, our utter disapproval of the too frequent instances, in which some of ourselves have occasionally entered among the people of other pastoral charges than their own, we need not say without the consent and even in opposition to the known wishes of those in charge—which, nevertheless, is true of the cases referred to—but in a way, if not for the purpose, of promoting strife and discord. Till appropriate discipline, or what we could more earnestly desire, a returning sense of propriety on their part, shall correct these disorders, we exhort you, beloved brethren, as many as love and pray for the peace and harmony of our Zion, to unite with us, in giving your decided discountenance to all such unbrotherly and un-methodistic movements.

It pains us that our sense of responsibility, constrains this reference to matters of so unseemly a character. It will be occasion of gratitude to you, as it is to us, to know that blameworthiness herein, attaches, as we are willing to believe, to but comparatively few. As far as our lay brethren are concerned, in any of the forestated departures from the discipline and order of our church, we have no difficulty in persuading ourselves that it is more the result of influences acting upon their sympathies, than of any original proclivity on their part to a spirit of disloyalty or innovation;—and that, as soon as they are disabused of false impressions, touching the character and aims of those from whom they suppose themselves to differ, their judgments and feelings will return to that channel in which they were accustomed to flow in harmony with our own. May the God of peace hasten the day when they and we shall have occasion to exclaim, in grateful concert—"Behold how good and how pleasant a thing it is, for brethren to dwell together in unity."

In our preceding counsels, we have confined ourselves mainly to subjects which, from the peculiar delicacy of their character, have seemed to demand our *united*, rather than our *individual* attention.   Of others, such as neglect of the social means of grace, and the sacraments of the church; non-attention to family worship, including the religious training and discipline of children; worldliness of spirit and conduct; not " going on to perfection;" want of practical sympathy with the great educational and religious enterprises of the church,—of these, if we do not now speak to you more at length, it is not because we have lost our conviction of their importance; but rather because we hold them in such consideration as to make them the topics of our ordinary and frequent pastoral admonitions.

And now, brethren, dearly beloved, and longed for, it were inexcusable remissness, not to notice, as matter of congratulation and thankfulness to the great Head of the church, the widely diffused influence of the Holy Spirit during the recent year.   Many souls in the various departments of the general church of Christ, and more or less in nearly all our charges, have been saved, and called with a holy calling.   At the same time, our membership have been largely quickened in the pursuit of that holiness, "without which no man shall see the Lord."

On the whole, we can never cease from fervent thanksgiving to the God and Father of our Lord Jesus Christ, for that state of salvation to which He has called you, and wherein you stand.   Losing sight of the local and exceptional, we thank Him for your steadfast adherence to our doctrines, discipline, and usages; your social harmony; your care for the instruction and salvation of the children of the church; together with your loyalty to that ministry, and those ordinances and institutions, so eminently instrumental in making us, instead of a weak, a *mighty people*, whose past history —if we remain united, and true to Methodism and to ourselves—shall prove prophetic of a future, whose glory will blend with the glories of that MILLENIUM day when all shall know the Lord, from the least to the greatest.